bratz™
MODEL FRIENDSHIP

PUFFIN BOOKS

Published by the Penguin Group
Penguin Books Ltd, 80 Strand, London WC2R 0RL, England
Penguin Group (USA) Inc., 375 Hudson Street, New York, New York 10014, USA
Penguin Group (Canada), 90 Eglinton Avenue East, Suite 700, Toronto, Ontario, Canada M4P 2Y3
(a division of Pearson Penguin Canada Inc.)
Penguin Ireland, 25 St Stephen's Green, Dublin 2, Ireland (a division of Penguin Books Ltd)
Penguin Group (Australia), 250 Camberwell Road, Camberwell, Victoria 3124, Australia
(a division of Pearson Australia Group Pty Ltd)
Penguin Books India Pvt Ltd, 11 Community Centre, Panchsheel Park, New Delhi – 110 017, India
Penguin Group (NZ), cnr Airborne and Rosedale Roads, Albany, Auckland 1310, New Zealand
(a division of Pearson New Zealand Ltd)
Penguin Books (South Africa) (Pty) Ltd, 24 Sturdee Avenue, Rosebank,
Johannesburg 2196, South Africa

Penguin Books Ltd, Registered Offices: 80 Strand, London WC2R 0RL, England

www.penguin.com

First published in the USA by Grosset & Dunlap, a division of Penguin Young Readers Group 2005
First published in Great Britain in Puffin Books 2005

4

Text copyright © TM and © 2005 MGA Entertainment, Inc. Bratz and all related logos, names and
distinctive likenesses are the exclusive property of MGA Entertainment, Inc.
All rights reserved

The moral right of the author and illustrator has been asserted

Made and printed in England by Clays Ltd, St Ives plc

Except in the United States of America, this book is sold subject to the condition that it shall not, by
way of trade or otherwise, be lent, re-sold, hired out, or otherwise circulated without the publisher's
prior consent in any form of binding or cover other than that in which it is published and without a
similar condition including this condition being imposed on the subsequent purchaser

British Library Cataloguing in Publication Data
A CIP catalogue record for this book is available from the British Library

ISBN 0–141–32042–7

bratz™

MODEL FRIENDSHIP

By Nancy Krulik

PUFFIN

chapter one

Flash!

Jade blinked with surprise as a flashbulb went off right in front of her face. "Cut it out, Koby," she moaned. "You're making me crazy with that digital camera of yours. You've been snapping pictures all day. I came to the mall to shop—not to go blind."

Jade's best friends, Cloe, Yasmin, and Sasha all laughed. "That's our Kool Kat," Yasmin teased. "Always the drama queen." The girls all called Jade Kool Kat both because she loved cats, and because there was no one cooler than Jade.

"You won't go blind," Koby assured her. But he put the camera away anyway.

Jade leaned back triumphantly in her seat, took a long sip of her strawberry-banana smoothie, and checked out the action going on around her in the food court.

"Boys can be so immature," she purred.

"Yeah, but who wants to grow up?" Koby countered.

"Koby's going to use that camera to take pictures for the *Stiles Shout-Out!*," Yasmin explained, referring to her "Daily Doings" column in the school newspaper. "He's got to keep up his photography chops."

"You aren't going to put *that* picture in the paper, are you?" Jade begged Yasmin. She sat up straight, suddenly concerned. "I wasn't ready for it." She turned to Koby. "I've a much better pose you can use," she told him as she flipped back her jet-black straight hair and flashed a huge smile. She looked just like a fashion model on the cover of a magazine. Koby obediently snapped another picture.

"She's just upset because you didn't give her a chance to fix her hair before you took her picture," Koby's pal Cameron teased. "You know how girls can be."

Sasha put her hands on her hips and stared defiantly at Cameron. "In the first place, Jade's hair is awesome. And so is her look." She pointed to Jade's funky embroidered jeans and far-out silver glitter platform boots. "In the second place, it's not just girls who have a passion for fashion. Check out Dylan over there."

All eyes turned toward the dude in question. But Dylan didn't notice that everyone was staring at him. He was too busy checking out his hair flair in the window of a nearby store. Everyone else began to laugh. Their giggles got his attention. "What's so funny?" Dylan asked.

"Oh, nothing," Koby teased as he snapped a shot of Dylan. "Photos are great. They capture a moment."

"Mmm . . . photos are nice, I guess," Cloe agreed. "But I'm more into portraits. I think an artist can capture just as wonderful an image as a photographer can." She used her perfectly-manicured fingers to lift up a sketch of Jade she'd just made on a napkin. Cloe was always drawing something. Even her math notebook was filled with more sketches than algebraic equations.

"That's an amazing sketch," Yasmin complimented Cloe as she studied the small pencil drawing. "It really looks like Jade. You even drew the earrings and the necklace she's wearing."

"I'd never draw Jade without her jammin' jewels," Cloe agreed. "The sketch isn't finished yet, but I think it looks a lot like Kool Kat." She turned to Koby. "And I didn't even need an expensive digital camera. All I needed was a pencil, paper, and talent."

"True," Koby agreed. "But photography takes talent, too. And you can't sketch a picture this fast!" He snapped a quick pic of Cloe. Then he moved the camera from his eye and studied the image of Cloe that immediately appeared on the square screen on the back of the camera.

Sasha peered over Koby's shoulder. "Oh, that's a nice one, Angel," she told Cloe. All of Cloe's friends called her Angel because she was so incredibly kind and caring. Of course, they also knew that if someone bugged one of her pals, this angel could get a real attitude. That was one of the great things about Cloe. She always had your back.

Cameron glanced over at the image in the camera. There was Cloe, her long blonde hair pulled back to reveal her big blue eyes opened wide with surprise. "It really is a good picture of you," Cam assured Cloe.

"I can print it out wallet-sized, if you want," Koby teased.

Jade, Sasha, Yasmin, and Dylan all laughed. Cameron and Cloe both blushed. It was kind of obvious that Cameron had a thing for Cloe—even though he'd never admit it.

Sasha took one last sip of her soda. "Okay, I'm done," she announced, hopping to her feet and tossing out her cup. "What do you guys say we get started on our latest shopping expedition?"

"Sounds good to me!" Jade agreed, hopping up from her seat. "I'm dying to check out that new boutique on the second floor."

"Me, too," Yasmin agreed. "I heard the store is the coolest."

"Not yet it isn't, Pretty Princess," Sasha disagreed. The girls all called Yasmin Pretty Princess because as far as they were concerned, Yasmin totally ruled!

"It's not?" Yasmin asked, confused. "But I heard . . ."

"It won't be the coolest until we shop there!" Sasha corrected her. She reached up and adjusted the cherry-red beanie perched on the top of her head. "Okay, gang. On your mark . . . get set . . . SHOP!"

"After you, Bunny Boo!" Cloe told her hip-hop-lovin' pal.

The girls hadn't gone two feet before Cameron found a different shop he wanted to check out. "I need to hit the electronics store," he told the others. "I've gotta find a new CD player to install in my dad's car."

"Can't we check out the new boutique first?" Yasmin asked. "I really can't wait to see it!"

"But the Soundaround is right here," Koby pointed out, indicating the entrance to the store.

Cam added, "And, besides, I . . ."

"We know. You're not as into clothes as the rest of us," Dylan finished Cameron's sentence.

Cam blushed. "It's not that I don't like clothes," he assured his pal. "It's just that I'm more into cars."

"I can tell," Dylan teased, checking out the flannel shirt and plain jeans his friend had thrown on to go to the mall.

"Don't worry, Dylan," Jade said, playfully running her fingers through Cameron's hair to spike it up a bit. "We're working on him. Someday, he'll be as fashion forward as you are."

"Not possible," Dylan joked, checking out his own outfit in the window of the electronics store.

"How about this?" Sasha suggested, finally. "We'll make a stop at the Soundaround now, as long as you guys all agree to shop at the new boutique."

"It's all right with me . . . if it's okay with Koby and Dylan," Cam agreed.

"Cool with us," Dylan assured the others.

"I guess that'll be okay," Yasmin agreed reluctantly. "But we're definitely hitting the boutique next!"

"Absolutely," Sasha assured her. She looked at the others. "Okay, gang, first stop, the Soundaround," Sasha said, taking Cameron by the hand and strolling into his favorite electronics store.

"Check out this CD player," Cloe said as the group made their way over to the car stereo aisle. "It's bright blue! That'll look awesome with the black leather in your dad's car."

"And it takes five platters at once," Yasmin added, reading the tag on the side of the machine.

"That's all great, but how does it sound?" Jade asked.

"Only one way to find out," Sasha replied. She reached over and turned on the model car stereo.

Immediately, a hip-hop beat—heavy on the bass, of course—began to blare from the speakers.

"Awesome," Sasha said as her body began to move. She snapped her fingers, and twirled around in a wild circle. Her friends all stared as Sasha let loose, dancing her heart out right in the middle of the store. "I can't help it," she told the others. "When I hear a beat, I gotta move my feet."

"I'm with you," Jade agreed. Then she, too, started dancing to the beat. Cloe, Cam, and Yasmin weren't about to let Sasha and Jade have all the fun. They got out on the floor and danced, too. At the same time, Koby pulled out his camera and began snapping candid photos of the girls and guys bopping to the beat of the hip-hop music that blared from the stereo. It didn't take long for some of the other teens in the store to join in the fun, as well. Soon, the whole aisle was filled with hip-hoppin' teens.

"Hey, it's like a party," Dylan shouted over the music.

"Wherever we go, it's a party," Jade agreed.

"We *are* the party," Yasmin added.

"Totally!" Koby agreed as he snapped a pic of Yasmin.

"Hey, that gives me an idea for some lyrics," Sasha mused. She bopped her head up and down a few times just to catch the rhythm, and then began to belt out her own rap. "Wherever we go, whatever we do, we stick together just like glue. We bring the fun, we bring the flair, a place without us is just nowhere!"

"Oh, yeah!" Jade shouted.

Unfortunately, the manager of the Soundaround wasn't as into partying as the kids were. The manager had no intention of letting his electronics store turn into a hot new club.

"May I help you?" he asked pointedly, turning the stereo off and glaring at the kids.

The room grew quiet. The friends all looked up at the store manager. He was a tall, older man with just a wisp of hair on his head, which he'd combed over his scalp to hide the fact that he was balding. He was wearing a button-down shirt that was missing a button in the middle, and his pants were hemmed somewhere above his ankles.

Jade giggled quietly. This guy needed a total makeover.

But now was obviously not the time to suggest that. The manager of the store seemed really upset.

"I was, just, um . . . I was looking for a CD player for my dad's car," Cameron stammered nervously. "I er . . . I . . . sort of wanted to hear what this one sounded like."

"I see," the manager said. "Did you like what you heard? You were just listening to one of our finest car stereos."

"It was okay," Sasha butted in. "But you can't make this kind of decision quickly. Cam's dad is going to be cruising around with his system for a long time. We'll have to listen to some more car stereos before we decide which one Cameron should get."

The manager's face grew pale.

"Don't worry. We're not going to listen to any more stereos now," Cloe assured him.

"Yeah, we've got more important things to shop for," Jade added.

"And that would be . . . ?" the store manager asked.

"Clothes, of course," Sasha told him.

"Funky clothes," Jade added.

"Oh, yeah!" Cloe agreed.

"You see, we love our music," Yasmin explained to the out-of-touch store manager. "But fashion is our passion."

"Which is why we're out of here," Dylan added.

"There's a new boutique upstairs that's just waiting for us to put our stamp of approval on it!" Jade said.

"See you later!" Sasha waved good-bye as the gang raced out of the store.

chapter two

"All right! That's exactly what I was looking for!" Yasmin squealed as she ran into the Unique Boutique and grabbed a chocolate-brown suede halter top from a shelf. "I told you this place was supposed to be the coolest."

"You weren't kidding," Cloe agreed as she held a zebra-print skirt up against her body and looked in the mirror. "I can't wait to try this on."

Sasha placed a blue floppy hat on her head. "What do you guys think? Is it me?"

"Totally hip-hop, Bunny Boo," Jade assured her. "It has your name on it."

"What about you?" Sasha asked Jade. "Anything here far-out enough?"

Jade strolled around the store, looking. She spotted a pair of jeans that were decorated with rows and rows of electric yellow fringe from the knees on down.

"These'll do," she told Sasha.

Quickly, the girls raced into the dressing rooms. They threw off their clothes and tried on new outfits.

Yasmin was the first to emerge from behind the curtain. She smiled as she studied her reflection in the mirror. The chocolate-brown suede of the halter top brought out her eyes. The long denim skirt with the lacing up the sides gave the outfit the Bohemian flair she adored.

"Pretty Princess," Sasha said as she emerged. "That look is awesome."

"So's yours," Yasmin complimented Sasha, eyeing the low-slung jeans and tube top Sasha was wearing.

Just then, Cloe emerged from her dressing room. "Angel, you look . . . angelic," Sasha gasped. Indeed, Cloe did look heavenly in her soft, sky blue, fuzzy tank top and glittery white skirt.

But it was Jade who left the others speechless. Once again, Kool Kat had taken a big fashion risk. And, once again, it had paid off. She looked beyond cool in her fringed jeans, yellow faux fur vest, and blue-and-yellow cowboy hat.

"Jade, you're so hip it hurts," Sasha squealed, giving her pal the ultimate compliment.

"Yeah, that look is mean to the x-treme!" Cloe agreed.

Jade smiled. "This is my kind of afternoon—setting fashion trends and hangin' with my friends."

The girls weren't the only ones trying on new outfits. Cameron and Dylan were busy checking out the guys' department with equal enthusiasm.

Cameron grabbed a loose-fitting gray jacket and threw it on over his shirt and jeans. "Whaddaya think?" he asked Dylan.

"Sweet." Dylan gave his approval. "It's cool and casual, just like you."

Dylan walked over to a display of rugby shirts in all different colors and studied the black-and-yellow striped shirts, the red-and-white striped shirts, and the green-and-blue striped shirts.

"What're you doing?" Cameron asked him.

"Deciding which lucky shirt will get to ride on my body," Dylan joked.

"Why don't you just buy them all?" Cam suggested.

"That's why you're one of my best buds," Dylan said as he scooped up three shirts. "Great minds think alike."

No doubt about it, most of the group were in their element. There was only one member who didn't seem too interested. Koby stood to the side, watching as his pals raced in and out of dressing rooms, trying on outfits. He didn't really feel like shopping. He was in the mood to head out to the park to take a few more photos. Koby moved slowly toward the door, hoping to be able to sneak out of the boutique without the others noticing.

But before Koby could take one step out of the store, Cloe and Yasmin grabbed him by the arms and dragged him to the guys' department of the shop.

"Oh, no you don't," Yasmin warned him. "We had a deal. We went to the electronics store, and now you get a new fashion look." Before Koby had any idea what was happening, Sasha, Jade, Yasmin, and Cloe were throwing clothes at him.

"Try these leather jeans," Jade suggested playfully.

"I don't think they're my style . . ." Koby insisted.

"You don't get any say," Sasha reminded him.

"We're the fashion experts. You just have to sit back and enjoy the ride."

Koby sighed. "Enjoy the ride," he muttered, reaching up and examining something on a nearby shelf.

"Just go with it, dude," Dylan suggested. "You know there's no beating these girls when they've teamed up."

"And we're always teamed up," Sasha added. "It's all for one and one for all." She plopped a baseball cap on Koby's head and turned it around so the brim faced the back.

"Oooh, check out the paisley shirt," Jade said. "It's so retro!"

"Retro's the way to go," Yasmin agreed. She pulled a peace sign medallion from off the counter. "You have to wear this with the paisley," she told Koby.

"I don't know about retro," Sasha said. "I think Koby should go with something more now." She handed him a black tank top, a tan photographer's vest, a funky tan-and-black beanie, and a pair of boots.

"Whoa, slow down, girl," Cloe warned. "I think Koby should try something a little less intense." She handed him a polo shirt and a pair of cargo pants.

Koby went into the dressing room with his arms overflowing with pants, shirts, hats, and shoes. "I don't even know which ones to try on first," he called out from behind the curtain.

"Just put on whatever seems comfortable," Cloe suggested.

"My own clothes seem comfortable," Koby replied.

"Other than that," she ordered.

A few moments later, Koby emerged from the dressing room.

"Whoa, dude, is that really you?" Dylan asked him. "Sweeeeeeet."

"Koby, you look like a movie star," Sasha exclaimed.

Koby grinned. He knew he looked good. And he felt comfortable in the green-and-brown camouflage jeans, short-sleeved brown tee, and camouflage-colored baseball cap he was wearing.

"I'm speechless," Angel told him. "That outfit is perfect. Which one of us gave you those clothes to try on?"

"None of you," Koby said. "I put them together

myself. While you guys were looking at retro clothes, funky clothes, and cargos, I grabbed these off the shelf."

"You're kidding," Cloe exclaimed.

"Nope," Koby assured her. He laughed when he saw the shocked expressions on his friends' faces. "Don't look so surprised, you guys. I can clean up when I want to."

"And you clean up real nice," Jade assured him. She looked down at her electric green watch. "Whoa, check out the time. I've gotta get going. We have that math test tomorrow and I haven't even started to study."

"Me, neither," Sasha added. "Let's pay for this stuff and take off."

It doesn't take fashion divas like Yasmin, Cloe, Sasha, and Jade long to change. Within minutes, the girls were at the cashier's counter with their new designer duds in hand.

The woman behind the counter smiled brightly at the four girls. "Are any of you interested in entering the Unique Boutique's Signature Style Model Contest?" she asked.

Jade's eyes lit up. "Model Contest?"

The woman nodded. "We're looking for a girl to represent our store in print ads. The winner gets to be in all the hottest fashion magazines."

"Why don't you just hire a professional model?" Yasmin asked.

"We're looking for a fresh face. Just a typical girl . . . with a not-so-typical sense of style."

"That's me," Jade assured the woman, holding up the faux fur vest she was purchasing.

"Oh, it's not me you have to convince," the cashier told her. "We're going to have a big competition with professional photographers and stylists doing all the judging. So far, we have about twenty-five girls who've entered."

Jade wasn't the kind of girl who could easily be intimidated. The large number of entrants didn't faze her one bit. "Where do I sign up?" she asked.

The cashier handed her a form. "Take this home and fill out all the information. Then mail it back to us with a photograph of yourself. Someone from the store will call you with all the details about the contest."

Jade took the form from the woman. "Thanks so much. I'll fill this form out right away. And I think I have just the perfect photo for you."

Cameron, Dylan, and Koby walked up to the counter. "What form?" Koby asked her.

"She's signing up for a modeling contest," Sasha explained.

"And I'm going to need that photo you took of me before . . . the good one, not the one you took when I wasn't looking," Jade told Koby.

Koby laughed. "I knew this camera would come in handy," he said.

"Do any of you other girls want to sign up?" the cashier asked.

"Don't look at me," Yasmin replied. "I've got too much to do. I have to write one column a week for the school paper. That takes up any free time I have."

"I'm not interested, either," Sasha agreed. "Modeling's not my thing. That's Jade's department. Always has been."

The girls laughed. That was the understatement of the century. Jade had never been shy about her modeling aspirations. She even cut out pictures of herself and glued them to the covers of her fave fashion mags, pretending to be the supermodel on the cover.

Dylan turned to Cloe. "How 'bout you, Cloe?" he asked. "Are you going to enter the contest?"

Cloe shook her head. "No. Jade's entering the contest. We should all stand behind her. I'd rather root for her than be part of a big competition."

Cameron looked at Cloe. There was nothing in her expression that would lead anyone to believe that she was being anything but truthful. Still, there was something in her voice that made him suspect that she would have loved to enter that contest—if Jade hadn't beaten her to it. But Cam didn't say anything. He just stood quietly in line and waited for his turn to pay.

As the kids left the store, Cameron pulled Koby aside. "Listen, I'd like a copy of that photo you took of Cloe," he whispered to his pal.

Koby smiled. "I knew it," he said. "You like her."

Cameron blushed. "She's just my friend," he assured Koby.

"Whatever you say," Koby replied with a smirk. "I'll get you the photo tomorrow."

chapter three

"Cloe, I love having sleepovers at your house," Yasmin said as she painted a bright lavender stripe on her big toe. "You have the best nail polish colors."

"I mixed that one myself," Cloe told her. "There just wasn't anything at the store that I liked. And you know me. I'm all about color."

It was a week after the mega shop-a-thon at the mall, and the girls were all gathered at Cloe's house for another one of their fave activities—a slumber party.

"Jade, can I borrow your yellow sweater for the dance next month?" Sasha asked.

"You mean the sweater I'm going to be wearing?" Jade replied. "I don't think so. But you can wear my silver-and-black miniskirt."

"Awesome," Sasha exclaimed. "It'll go perfectly with my new black suede beanie and my platform boots."

"I was thinking of wearing my new Funk 'N' Glo jeans to the dance," Yasmin mentioned.

"Then you have to check out this nail polish," Cloe said, holding out her hand. "It glows in the dark. It would be perfect with those jeans."

The girls gathered to look at Cloe's nails. They were incredible! Not only had she brushed on a layer of the glow-in-the-dark polish, she'd also managed to paint a hot pink rose on each of her nails.

"Leave it to Angel to use her nails as teeny tiny paint canvases," Jade teased. She leaped up excitedly. "Do you think you could paint something on my nails next weekend?"

"Sure," Cloe agreed. "How about little cat prints?"

"Purrrrr-fect," Kool Kat agreed.

"But what's so special about next weekend?"

Jade folded her long, lean legs underneath her. Her eyes grew wide with excitement. "I've got huge news. I heard from Unique Boutique. They called me just before I came over here. The first round of the modeling competition is next weekend."

"The first round?" Yasmin asked.

"Uh-huh. There are going to be three elimination rounds. The first competition is the hair and make-up contest. They've hired some real make-up artists to judge that one. Then, all the girls who make it to the next round will be photographed. Real magazine editors will choose the winners of that competition. The final competition is for style. Each girl has to come up with her own original outfit."

"You'll win that one hands down," Sasha assured her. "No one has a better sense of style than our Kool Kat."

"I've got to get to the third round first, Bunny Boo," Jade reminded her.

"Once those judges see you, they'll forget there's anyone else in the contest," Sasha assured Jade.

"So what time are we going to sleep?" Yasmin asked, pulling on one of her turquoise fluffy slippers.

"Who sleeps at a sleepover?" Sasha asked her. She took a bite out of a peanut butter-chocolate chip cookie. "We're staying up all night."

"Aren't you guys the least bit tired?" Yasmin yawned. "I know I am."

"It's still early. I don't want to crash out," Jade said.

"Oh, we're not sleeping," Sasha assured her. "In fact, I'm going to scare Yasmin awake! It's ghost story time."

Cloe grinned. "Great!" she exclaimed.

"Bunny Boo'll make sure you don't fall asleep," Jade assured Yasmin. "She tells the best scary stories."

"Okay, but take it easy on me," Yasmin said. "Last time you told a ghost story, I didn't sleep for three days."

Sasha laughed. "Okay," she promised. Then she lowered her voice almost to a whisper. "It all began on a dark and stormy night . . ."

"Doesn't it always?" Jade asked. "How come scary stories never begin on a sunny day?"

"What's scary about a sunny day?" Sasha asked. Once again, she lowered her voice and began to whisper into the darkness. "Thunder and lightning crashed wildly in the sky. Most people in the small New England town were huddled together inside their small cottages. But two girls were stuck outside, forced to wait out the storm in the tiny campsite they'd constructed in the nearby woods.

They'd been camping, and they hadn't had a chance to leave before the storm started. Now it was too dangerous to try and find their way out of the woods. The forest was dark and foreboding. The rain had put the fire out, and the storm clouds blocked the moon. The only light came from the zigzagging flashes of lightning overhead. The trees, which had once seemed so beautiful and welcoming, now looked like monsters, with their branches reaching out ominously like bony arms ready to grab the girls at any moment. The rain pounded on the girls' tiny tent. The thunder crashed above. And then, suddenly, they heard a noise . . ."

Brrrring . . .

"Aaaaahhhhhhhhhhhhh," Yasmin, Cloe, and Jade all screamed out at once.

Brrrring . . .

Sasha laughed and flicked on the light. "Relax, you guys. It's just the phone." She picked up the receiver. "Hello?"

"Is this Cloe?" a woman's voice asked.

"No. I'll get her for you." Sasha held out the phone.

"Angel, it's for you."

"Can you put it on speaker?" Cloe asked. "My nails are still wet."

Sasha nodded and pushed the speakerphone button.

"Hello?" Cloe said.

"Is this Cloe?"

"Yes."

"Hi. I'm calling from the Unique Boutique. I'm sorry to be contacting you so late in the evening, but I have a very long list of girls to contact."

"Contact?" Cloe asked. "For what?"

"I wanted to let you know that the first round of our modeling competition begins next Saturday," the woman from the boutique continued. "You need to come with your face freshly washed. We'll provide the make-up for you to apply."

A confused look came over Cloe. "But I didn't enter the contest," she said.

"I'm looking at your application right here, dear," the woman said. "It's got your photo, address, and telephone number right here. How else could I have contacted you?"

"But . . ."

"I'd love to chat, but I have several more phone calls to make. See you Saturday." And, with that, the woman hung up the phone. The line went dead.

All the girls turned and stared at Cloe. Jade looked as though she was about to cry. "How could you?!" she asked in a sad, hurt voice.

"I didn't!" Cloe assured her.

Jade studied her friend's face. "Why would you do this?" she asked her. "You know how much I want to win this contest."

"Honest, Jade. I would never want to compete against you."

Cloe had never lied to Jade before. But Jade refused to believe her. And the thought of Cloe lying to her made her even more angry than the idea that she'd entered the contest behind her back. "You bet you wouldn't," Jade snapped at her. "You could never beat me."

Cloe's eyes opened wide. "Excuse me?" she said.

"You heard me."

Sasha leaped up. "Come on, you guys, calm down.

It's just a contest. We're all friends here."

"A contest I entered first," Jade reminded her. "Some friend. She didn't even have the guts to tell me she'd entered it."

"I didn't enter," Cloe insisted again.

"Then how did they get your application?" Jade demanded.

"I don't know."

"Come on, Jade," Yasmin said. "You know Angel would never lie. If she says she didn't enter this contest, then she didn't enter the contest."

"Someone must have mailed the entry form in for me," Cloe deduced.

"But you had to attach a photo to the form. Who has a picture of you?" Jade demanded.

"Lots of people," Cloe said. "We all have pictures of each other."

"Well, I certainly didn't put in an entry form for you." Jade looked pointedly at Sasha and Yasmin. "Did either of you?"

The girls shook their heads.

"So there you go," Jade said. "You must have done it, Cloe."

"I didn't," Cloe insisted again. "I swear."

"Think, Cloe," Sasha butted in. "Does anyone else have a photo of you?"

Yasmin jumped up. "Koby!"

"What does he have to do with anything?" Jade asked her.

"Koby has a picture of Cloe," she said. "He took it at the mall with his new camera." Yasmin raced over to the phone and hurriedly dialed Koby's number.

"Hello?" he said as he answered the phone.

"Koby, did you enter Cloe in that modeling contest at the mall?" Yasmin demanded.

"Hi to you, too, Yasmin," Koby said.

"Oh, sorry," Yasmin apologized. "Hi, Koby. I didn't mean to be rude. It's just that this is an emergency."

"An emergency that involves a modeling contest?" he asked. He sounded very confused.

"Yeah," Yasmin replied. "I need to know right away if you sent in an application and a photo of Cloe."

"Why would I do that?"

"I don't know," Yasmin said. "But somebody did. We're just trying to figure out who it was. Whoever entered her in the contest had to have a picture of her. You took that shot of her in the food court, remember?"

"Sure," Koby recalled. "That was a great picture. Cameron loved it so much, he asked for a copy of it. He said it made Cloe look like a model."

Cameron! The girls all looked at one another. "That's it!" Yasmin exclaimed. "Thanks, Koby," she said into the speakerphone.

"No prob," Koby replied.

"Night," Yasmin said as she pushed the speakerphone button to off. She looked at her friends. "Well, another mystery solved."

Sasha looked at Jade. "I think you owe Angel an apology."

Jade nodded and reached over to give Cloe a hug. "I'm sorry," she said sincerely.

"It's okay," Cloe said.

"It was just that I want this so badly," Jade said.

"And I think I have a shot at winning. But when I thought you were going to be competing against me . . . well, that could make it close, you know. But as long as you're not going to be in the contest . . ."

"Who says I'm not?" Cloe asked her. "Now that they have my application, maybe I will."

"But you didn't enter," Jade said.

"I know. But now I sort of want to do it. You made it sound like so much fun. I'd like to meet all those experts. I bet they'll give some great fashion advice."

Jade frowned. *Me and my big mouth*, she thought ruefully to herself. Now she was going to have to compete against Cloe. And Angel could be tough competition. "I don't think it's your kind of thing," Jade said quickly, trying to discourage her friend.

"How come?"

"Well, you never said anything about being a model before. And now probably wouldn't be a great time for you to start."

"Why not?" Cloe asked.

"Because I'm going to be in it."

Cloe looked Jade straight in the eye. Ordinarily, she would've pulled out of the contest and backed Jade, just like she had at the mall, but Jade was acting so cocky. "Is there some rule that says two friends can't be in the same contest?"

"Jade, come on," Yasmin urged. "This is no reason to fight. You guys have been friends forever. Why let a competition come between you? Besides, think of it this way: It'll make it more fun to have a friend to share the experience with."

Cloe and Jade stared at each other. They looked like two Wild West outlaws preparing for a duel.

Sasha studied the looks on her friends' faces and sighed wearily. Fun? Somehow, she doubted it.

chapter four

"Wait until you hear my idea for how I want to wear my hair on Saturday!" Jade exclaimed as she slid in the seat beside Sasha in the school cafeteria on Monday. "I'm telling you, I'm going to make those judges sit up and take notice."

Sasha had no doubt of that. No one had hair flair like Jade did. Jade's funky trendsetting sense of style made *everyone* take notice. Sasha looked at her friend. At the moment, Jade was wearing a blue-and-white tie-dye tank top with lace along the edges. She'd matched it up with a pair of pale blue leather jeans. Jade had tied her hair high on her head in two long, dark ponytails. She looked adorable, but Sasha had a feeling that wasn't the way Jade was going to wear her hair for the contest. "What have you come up with?" she asked her excitedly.

"Well, I've been studying my face shape in the

mirror," Jade told Sasha. "You know, that's really the best way to pick a hairstyle. I mean, people with round faces probably should go with a little height at the crown of their heads to make their faces look longer. And people with square faces should try soft bangs to soften the angles of their faces. And girls with heart-shaped faces need to keep their hair chin-length and bouncy to add fullness to their narrow chins. Now me, I have an oval-shaped face . . ."

"I know, I know," Sasha said, obviously growing impatient waiting for Jade to unveil her plan.

Jade, however, was enjoying the suspense. "That means I'm lucky enough to be able to wear my hair any way I want. So, I've decided to go with an updo," Jade said, piling her pigtails on top of her head to give Sasha the general idea. "I think that's really glamorous."

"It totally is," Sasha agreed.

"But I just can't let my natural style slide," Jade continued. "So I think I'm going to add a streak of silver glitter to my hair."

"Oh, awesome," Sasha said, picturing Jade's dark hair accented with a streak of shimmering silver.

"The judges will love that!"

Jade nodded. "I think so, too. Of course, I'm going to need some funky earrings, since I'm putting my hair up and . . ." Jade looked up and stopped speaking suddenly. Cloe and Cameron had just appeared at the lunch table with trays in hand.

"Hi, Sasha," Cloe said. "Jade."

"Hey, girls. What's shakin'?"

"Nothin' but the Jell-O," Sasha laughed. "Grab a seat. Cam, you sit next to me. Angel, there's a chair right there, next to Jade."

Cloe shook her head. "That's okay, I'll sit right here," she said, taking a seat across the table from the other two girls. Cameron plopped down in the seat beside Cloe. That put him right across from Jade. Jade dropped her eyes and concentrated on the food sitting on her tray.

"I love your hat," Cloe said, pointing to the purple suede floppy hat Sasha was wearing on her head. Cloe raised her forefinger at Sasha's eye level.

The view of Cloe's unique manicure made Sasha squeal. Cloe's nails were all sky blue in color. But Cloe had painted palm trees and flowers on them, as well. "How cool is that?" Sasha exclaimed.

"I was just experimenting," Cloe said, waving her nails for all to see. Cameron laughed, and waved his nails in the air, as well. Unfortunately, his nails were slightly gray—he'd been fixing cars in auto shop, and he'd had trouble getting the grease out from under his nails.

"I don't think that's quite the look a Unique Boutique model might wear," Sasha giggled.

Cloe laughed. "Actually, I don't know how I'm going to do my nails. Although, grease underneath is not on my list of ideas. I was thinking about this all last night. It's not easy coming up with the perfect manicure plan for Saturday. The thing is, I haven't decided what dress to wear. And that'll determine what colors I'll paint my nails."

"What about that denim halter dress you found at that store by the beach?" Sasha suggested.

"Maybe," Cloe mused.

"Or you could wear your camouflage skirt and the green tank top. That one looks so hot on you," Sasha continued.

"I was thinking about that. Or maybe my . . ."

"Ahem," Cameron interrupted. He glanced in Jade's direction.

Cloe got the message loud and clear. She probably shouldn't be discussing this in front of Jade. She was, after all, the competition. How weird was that? Jade had always been one of her best friends. They told each other everything. And now she couldn't even discuss what dress she was going to wear with her. Cloe felt very uncomfortable all of a sudden. "Anyway, I'll probably decide that morning," Cloe finished up feebly. "And then I'll do my nails that day. At least that way my nails won't have time to get chipped before the judges can see them."

"Good idea," Sasha said. "Jade was just telling me that she's been working on hairstyles for Saturday. She's done all this research about face shapes and hairstyles and stuff. I'll bet she could help you work on that part of your look. And since you already promised that you'd do her nails, you could get together Saturday before the competition. That way, you guys would both be sure to make it to the next level."

"Oh, I don't know," Cloe said. "I was thinking that I might not have time to give Jade a manicure. Especially not on Saturday morning. I mean, you know how long it takes to do your nails—you've got to remove all the old polish, and file them, put on nail-strengthening cream, and remove all the cuticles. And that's before you even start with a base coat. I just don't see how I can do that for both of us."

"And hairstyles are tricky. It could take me a while to get together the one I just told you about," Jade added. "There's no way I'll have time to figure something out for Cloe, too."

Sasha sighed. "But you guys could really help each other. You always have in the past. Why should this be any different?"

Jade and Cloe looked at each other. Neither girl said a word. But from the looks on their faces, it was obvious that they wouldn't be sharing their expertise any time soon.

Just then, Koby and Yasmin entered the cafeteria carrying stacks of newspapers in their arms. They stopped to pile the papers in the bins that were located beside the cafeteria doors. Now, everyone in school could pick up a copy of the school newspaper on their way in or out of lunch.

When they were through, Yasmin took one copy of the paper and brought it over to the table where her friends were sitting. She plopped down beside Cam and opened the paper to page two. "Check out the new *Stiles Shout-Out!* My column is about the Unique Boutique's modeling contest!" She laid the paper out on the table so everyone could see. The headline read:

CLOE AND JADE ENTER MODELING COMPETITION
Stiles High Girls Represent the School

"Isn't it great?" she asked.

"No, it's not," Jade replied.

"What?" Yasmin asked. "This is a whole column about you and Cloe. I'm trying to get the whole school to support you guys in the contest."

"Well, it's obvious who you're rooting for," Jade said.

"I'm rooting for both of you," Yasmin insisted.

"Then why is Cloe's name first in the headline?" Jade demanded.

"I don't know," Yasmin admitted. "I guess I didn't

really think about it."

"Well, C does come before J," Koby suggested.

"Oh, so you're on her side," Jade said.

"Huh?" Koby asked. "Are we choosing sides now?"

"Apparently, we are," Cloe insisted. "And that's why Jade's picture is at the top of the page, while mine's all the way down here on the bottom."

"We just did that because her picture was horizontal and yours was vertical. We needed a horizontal shot under the headline, and a vertical one to finish out the last column," Yasmin explained.

"I think hers is bigger," Cloe insisted.

"B . . . B . . . But . . ." Yasmin began.

"Will you two listen to yourselves?" Sasha leaped to Yas's defense. "This is ridiculous. The four of us have always been really close. We've never let anything come between us. And now you guys are letting some stupid contest ruin everything. I just don't get it."

"You definitely don't," Jade agreed. "Or you wouldn't be calling it a stupid contest. This is very important to me."

"It's important to me, too," Cloe said.

Sasha sighed. "Well, it's nice to hear you two agree on something for a change."

Cloe smiled slightly at Sasha, but she still didn't agree to make up with Jade. "I gotta go," she said quickly. "I have English in a few minutes, and I need to study."

"I'm going, too," Jade said. "I was so busy working on my hair last night, I never finished the chapter we were supposed to read."

Just then, Dylan arrived at the table. He took a seat on the other side of Sasha. Just as he sat down, Cloe and Jade both leaped to their feet. The girls stormed out of the cafeteria—using separate exits.

Dylan watched as the girls left without even saying hello or good-bye to him. "Was it something I said?" he asked as they walked away.

■ ■ ■ ■

That night, Jade sat alone in her room, poring through piles and piles of blouses, skirts, jeans, shoes, dresses, vests, hats, and handbags, trying to put together one of her signature-style looks for the competition on Saturday. The first round of the contest was for hair and make-up, but Jade knew that she had to have just the right clothes, as well. This was the first time she would be meeting the judges—and the other girls in the competition. She wanted to make a good first impression. She also wanted the other girls to know just what kind of style queen they were up against. A little fashion intimidation never hurt.

Right now, Jade had eight different outfits put together. They were strewn across her bed, over her chair, and on the floor. But none of them made the statement she was looking for. To tell the truth, Jade was no closer to deciding what she was going to wear than she had been when her clothes were still in her closet.

Suddenly, she heard the muffled sound of her phone ringing. Obviously, the phone was hidden beneath one of the piles. The question was, which one? It sounded as though the ringing was coming from beneath a pile of brightly-colored sweaters. Quickly, Jade dug into the mound of wool and cotton, and pulled out her phone.

"Hello?" she said into the receiver.

"Jade, it's me, Cloe."

"I don't feel like talking right now," Jade answered. "I'm very busy."

Cloe sighed. "Look, I was thinking about what Sasha said today. You know, about letting a stupid contest get between us."

"It's not a stupid contest," Jade insisted.

"I agree," Cloe said. "But letting it break up our friendship is stupid."

Jade thought about that for a moment. A million memories flooded through her mind—her and Cloe at the beach, at the movies, and cruising around town in Cloe's convertible. She, Cloe, Sasha, and Yasmin had shared a whole lot of good times. "I guess you're right," Jade said finally.

"Sasha was the one who pointed it out," Cloe said in typical Angel fashion. She was unwilling to take credit for something her friend had figured out. "She always knows how to get to the heart of the issue."

"I know," Jade agreed. She paused for a moment.

"But you and I still have a huge problem that I don't think anyone—not even Bunny Boo—can solve."

"What's that?" Cloe asked.

"How can we be friends and still compete against each other?"

Both girls were quiet for a moment, trying to come up with a solution to such a difficult issue. Finally, Cloe broke the silence. "Look, it's okay for you to want to win. I want to win, too," she told Jade honestly. "But if I can't, I would want the Unique Boutique spokesmodel to be you."

"I guess I would want it to be you, too . . . if I didn't win, I mean," Jade replied slowly. "I'd rather have it be one of us than some stranger."

"Exactly what I was thinking," Cloe told her. "So here's my idea. Maybe you could sleep here Friday night, and I could do your nails first thing in the morning. I sketched out these tiny cat faces that are really adorable. I could paint them on your thumbs and . . ."

"I don't think so," Jade interrupted.

"What?" Cloe asked. "I thought you agreed that we could be friends and still . . ."

"I mean, I don't think you should do my nails Saturday morning," Jade answered. "You need to do them for me Friday night."

"Why?"

"Because I'll need them to be completely dry when I do your hair Saturday morning!"

"Oh, Kool Kat, would you really do my hair?" Cloe exclaimed.

"Sure I will," Jade assured her. "I think a French braid with a long strand of ribbon woven into it would look awesome on you."

"Oooh, that sounds perfect," Cloe agreed.

"I know," Jade laughed. "I can't wait to try it out on you."

"Then we're friends again?" Cloe asked cautiously.

"The very best," Jade assured her.

chapter five

By the time Cloe and Jade arrived at the boutique on Saturday morning, the store was already teeming with excited teenage girls. Cloe looked nervously at Jade. "Some of these girls are really gorgeous," she remarked.

Jade smiled confidently. "There are lots of gorgeous girls in the world, but no one has our style," she consoled her pal. "They also don't have our secret weapon."

"Our secret weapon?" Cloe asked. "It must be some secret. I don't even know what it is."

"Sure you do," Jade replied with a smile. "Our secret weapon is each other." She gave Cloe's hand a squeeze. "Some girls might have great hair, and some girls may have great manicures, but we're the only ones who have both."

Cloe looked down at her hand, which was still intertwined with Jade's. She could see both of their magnificent manicures—Jade's with the cat faces on her thumbs, and tiny black cat paw prints painted onto each of her other nails. Cloe could see the brightly colored rainbows on her own thumbs, and the sky-blue background with tiny white clouds she'd painted onto her other fingers. Then she thought about the magnificent French braid Jade had created for her. The bright blue ribbon Kool Kat had woven into the braid perfectly matched her halter dress. It was the best hairstyle in the room—with the exception of Jade's glimmering updo.

"You're right," Cloe agreed with Jade. "No one here can beat the two of us."

"It's all about teamwork," Jade agreed.

"All right, girls, let's get started," a tall, thin woman with perfectly-arched eyebrows, smooth creamy skin, and bright red lipstick called out.

The group of nervously giggling girls grew silent immediately. "As you all know by now, the first round of our competition will be focused on your personal make-up skills," the woman continued. "That's why we asked you to come with cleanly scrubbed faces. Our experts will provide you with some basic make-up tips. Then you will be responsible for implementing them on your own faces. You'll be judged on how well you create your own make-up palette. The judges will choose ten girls who they believe have the most professional looks. The winners of today's competition will go on to the second round. Unfortunately, since we are only choosing ten girls, many of you will be out of the competition today."

There was an audible murmur running through the crowd as the girls contemplated that possibility.

"But, don't worry, no one will go home empty-handed," the woman continued. "The girls who aren't chosen will still go home with a fifteen-dollar gift certificate to the Unique Boutique."

"That's a nice prize," Cloe whispered to Jade.

"What do you care?" Jade asked her. "We won't be going home with one of those today. We're moving on to the next phase of the competition. I can feel it."

"I hope you're right," Cloe replied.

"And now, let me introduce our make-up expert," the woman with the red lipstick said. "He's an internationally-acclaimed make-up artist who has worked with models worldwide. He's extremely knowledgeable about what photographers are looking for when they take their pictures."

A tall, thin man in a gray muscle shirt and jeans stood up in front of the room. "Hello, everyone," he said in a voice that had just a slight twinge of a southern accent. "It's a pleasure to be in the company of so many beautiful young women. But it takes more than beauty to be a model. It takes a certain magic that occurs between a girl and the camera lens. Some people have it, some people don't. But you can help make the magic happen by giving your face the lift make-up can provide." He smiled and sipped from his water bottle. "But before we start with make-up, let me give you all a tip. Great skin starts from within. No matter how much you wash your face, or how well you moisturize, the best way to keep your skin fresh and supple is to drink lots and lots of water. Not soda, not ice tea, not even juice. Water. It's nature's simplest beauty secret."

Instantly, several girls reached up and grabbed bottles of water from the table.

"Now that's a good start," he continued. "But water

can't do it all. With hot lights blaring on your face, and a camera threatening to give you a close-up at any point, you're going to have to get a little help from make-up. The make-up style you decide on will have a lot to do with the image you're trying to put forth. Some modeling jobs will require you to be more dramatic, while others will be looking for a softer, girl-next-door look. Today, we're going to let you decide which style works best for you. But don't get used to it. It's rare that a model gets to choose her own look."

Cloe looked over at Jade. Without even asking, she was certain that Kool Kat was going to go for a more extreme gleam than she was. Jade just wasn't the soft, girl-next-door type. Of course, she could probably pull that off if she wanted. Jade could do anything.

Frankly, Cloe didn't think Kool Kat needed much make-up at all to look gorgeous. Her exotic good looks spoke for themselves. In fact, sitting there with no make-up at all, Jade had managed to bring attention to herself. Cloe had already noticed many of the other girls eyeing Jade nervously. Somehow, they already knew that Jade would present them with some serious competition.

What Cloe didn't notice was that several of the girls were staring at her in exactly the same way. Her big blue eyes and peaches-and-cream complexion made her the perfect candidate for that girl-next-door look the make-up artist had alluded to. Both Jade and Cloe were stunning—in their own unique ways. But it wasn't their make-up, their hair, or even their clothes that made them gorgeous. Their true beauty came from within.

"Now, let's take a look at the make-up we have here," the man continued in his soft southern drawl. "If your skin is normal or a bit oily, your best bet is to start with a matte foundation. That'll make sure that your skin doesn't look too shiny. If you've got dry skin, try a liquid foundation instead. If you don't want to wear foundation, try a tinted face powder. Whether you choose powder or foundation, the most important thing to remember is to make sure it matches your own skin tone. And, speaking of matching—it's not a great idea to try and match your lip color to your outfit. Try to stick to a neutral shade, or a shade that lights up your face. You don't want your lipstick to overpower your overall look. Unless, of course, you're doing a commercial for lip color. Then the whole point is to have your lips be the first thing anyone notices."

The make-up artist continued talking to the girls, explaining techniques to make their eyes look bigger and their lips appear fuller, how to use blush and contour to make their cheekbones look higher, and when and where to use shimmer and body glitter. As he spoke, many of the girls took notes. One or two actually videotaped his speech. But Jade didn't need any of that. She was committing everything this man said to memory. As he spoke, her mind was going a mile a minute trying to figure out how she was going to use his suggestions to wow the judges with a look that stood out from the crowd.

It wasn't long before she was given the chance to try. After the make-up artist used a large doll's head to demonstrate the best way to blend three shades of eye shadow together, the woman with the bright red lipstick returned to the front of the room.

"Thank you so much," she said to the make-up artist. Then she turned to the girls. "Okay, ladies, this is your chance. We've gathered every color of eye shadow, mascara, eyeliner, lip liner, gloss, concealer, powder, and foundation you can imagine. They're all in the back of the store, right near the cashier. We've also lined up mirrors and dressing tables for each of you. Your mission is to come up with a look that works for you, and impresses our panel of make-up artists and modeling agency execs. Okay, girls, here we go. Ready, set . . . MAKE UP!"

That was all the encouragement the girls needed. They practically dove onto the make-up tables. For the next hour, brushes were flying, powder was puffing up into the air, and eye shadows, lip liners, and blushes of all colors were being applied with expert care.

Cloe decided to play up her sweet, angelic looks. She used pale blue eye shadow and a little bit of blue liner to play up her eyes. For her lips, she stuck to a neutral tone, but made sure to use plenty of gloss to make her mouth look especially kissable.

Jade, on the other hand, was busy playing up her exotic looks to the extreme. She experimented with face glitter, and gave her cheeks an especially shimmery glow. She made her eyes seem even bigger by only lining them from the corner to middle of her eye. And she used a light, shimmery eye shadow right under her eyebrows. When she was finished, Jade checked her reflection in the mirror. She smiled with confident appreciation for her appearance. Between the glitter in her hair, and the glitter under her brows, the judges were sure to recognize her for the shimmering star she was.

As Cloe glanced over at her friend, she was overcome with admiration. Not because Jade looked so amazing—Cloe was used to seeing Jade that way. Cloe was just incredibly impressed with the confidence that Jade exuded in everything she said or did. No one would ever argue with the fact that, in her own way, Cloe was every bit as gorgeous as Jade. But Cloe wasn't as certain of herself as Jade was. Still, looking at herself in the mirror right now, Cloe couldn't help but be pleased with her reflection. And no matter the outcome today, she knew she had learned a lot, and done her best.

"Okay, ladies, time is up," the woman with the bright red lips called out. "Please put down your make-up brushes and come stand here in front of the judges."

The aspiring models did as they were told. Jade was the first one up out of her seat. She positioned herself right in front of the table of judges, and smiled brightly in their direction.

Cloe tried to stand beside her friend, but she found it difficult to make her way through the crowd of girls, many of whom were trying to position themselves in the best possible light, and as close to the judges as possible.

It seemed like forever as the judges carefully studied the faces of the girls in front of them. Their pencils made scratching noises as they scribbled notes about each of the girls in their notepads. One of the judges walked slowly down the line of girls, eyeing each one close-up. As he strolled past Jade, she turned her head slightly, hoping the glitter in her hair and on her face would catch the light and make her sparkle at him. Cloe couldn't help but be impressed with her friend's ability to show herself off to the best possible advantage.

But showing off wasn't Cloe's style. Instead, she shook off her nervousness as best she could and gave the judge one of the warm, friendly smiles she was famous for.

She studied his face, hoping for some sign that he liked the way she had created a fresh look for herself, but the man's face was void of any emotion at all. He simply looked at each girl and scribbled something onto his pad without changing his expression.

As that judge took his seat, he whispered something to the two other judges. Soon, they were all whispering among themselves and exchanging notepads to show one another how they'd graded the girls. Finally, the woman with the red lipstick stood and faced the contestants.

"Well, let me say that you all look incredibly lovely," she assured the contestants. "It is obvious you've taken all of our make-up tips to heart, and used them to fit your own individual styles. I wish we could use all of you as our spokesmodels. But, unfortunately, many of you will be finishing your portion of the competition today. I am about to announce the names of the girls who will be moving on to phase two of our contest. Everyone, please save your squeals, shouts, and applause until I've called out all ten names."

Cloe glanced down the line at Jade. She seemed

perfectly calm . . . at least outwardly. But Cloe could tell Jade was anxious; she was twisting the first two fingers of her right hand together over and over again. It was a habit Kool Kat had when she was slightly stressed. Usually, it came out before science quizzes.

Cloe was really nervous, too. At first, she had entered the contest just for fun (and to teach Jade a lesson about being overconfident) but now that she was in the thick of it, she really wanted to win—or, at least, to get to the next level.

"Our first semifinalist is Jade," the woman with the red lips said. Jade's tense smile broke into a full-fledged grin as she took a step forward and stood just slightly in front of the line.

Cloe listened intently to hear if her name would also be called. But the next name wasn't hers, neither was the next, or the next. Before long, seven more names had been called and none of them was Cloe's. Cloe tried to keep up a brave front. She was proud of Jade for having made the cut, but it still hurt that she wasn't going to be . . .

"Our next semifinalist is Cloe," the woman with the

red lips announced, interrupting Cloe's thoughts.

At first, Cloe wasn't sure she'd heard her name. But when she saw the judges all smiling at her, she knew she'd made it to the next round. The woman with the red lips announced the name of one more semifinalist, but neither Cloe nor Jade heard who it was. They were too busy smiling at each other. Jade gave Cloe a thumbs-up sign. Cloe returned the signal.

"Okay, girls, that will be all. The contestants who were not chosen to move on to the next round can pick up their gift certificates at the cashier's table. I'd like to ask our semifinalists to please remain behind, so that we can give you each an appointment for your individual photo shoot. Your photos will be taken individually by a world-renowned photographer, and then displayed here next Saturday for our judges to see."

Cloe and Jade were both excited, and a bit nervous. Their one-two punch had obviously been a success in this round of the competition. There was no doubt that their hairstyles and manicures had complimented their individual make-up choices. And the fact that they each had a close friend there with them gave Cloe and Jade the confidence they needed to wow the judges. After all, there's nothing more beautiful than a girl who is confident about who she is. But the girls would not be together at their photo sessions. There would be no one there to cheer them on.

Would they both be able to move on to the third stage, or would one of them be left behind?

chapter six

"Koby! Just the man I wanted to see," Jade shouted as she raced to catch up with her pal on her way to school Monday morning.

"Hey, Kool Kat. Congrats on the big victory!"

Jade shook her head. "It's not a victory yet," she explained. "But I'm determined to make it one. And that's where you come in."

"Huh?"

"I need your photographic genius . . . and that incredible new camera of yours."

Koby laughed. "Oh, so now I'm a photographic genius. At the mall, you were ready to shove that incredible new camera down my throat."

"That was different," Jade told him. "I wasn't ready for you to take my photo. But now, I have to be ready for anything a photographer throws at me. I need you to take a bunch of practice shots of me, so that I can figure out which is my best side, how I should wear my hair, and all of that."

Koby shrugged. "Sure, I'll take some test shots of you," he said. "But just so you know, this is a digital camera. The photographer you're working with may be using a traditional camera, and film."

"That's okay," Jade assured him. "I just want to be able to see how my hair and make-up look, and a digital camera can show me that right away. Besides, lots of professional photographers use digital cameras now. That way, they can send the photos via computer to magazines."

"Okay, you've convinced me," Koby laughed. "How about tomorrow afternoon?"

"What's wrong with today after school?" Jade asked. She showed Koby the huge furry knapsack she'd slung across her back. "I have lots of make-up with me, and my electric hair straightener, too. And I have tons of outfits in my locker to choose from."

Koby laughed. It was common knowledge that Jade had an entire wardrobe stashed away in that locker of hers.

But that didn't mean that he could just drop everything to take her picture. He already had other plans. "I'm taking test shots of Cloe today, Kool Kat," Koby explained.

"Oh, she asked you, too?" Jade said, her voice sounding just a bit annoyed.

"Sure. She called me from her cell phone Saturday, right after she left the mall," Koby told her. "I figured you knew. You guys tell each other everything, don't you?"

"Usually," Jade muttered through gritted teeth. She frowned. For all her talk about teamwork, Cloe had sure kept this a secret. Jade felt angry and betrayed . . . for a minute. Then she realized that she wasn't exactly planning on telling Cloe about her own plan to have Koby take a few practice shots, either. It wasn't easy remaining best friends with your competitor, after all.

■ ■ ■ ■

Jade's appointment with the real photographer was on Wednesday afternoon. She spent all Tuesday night studying the test shots Koby had taken of her. Jade knew that photographers used very bright lights in their studios, and she was worried that she wouldn't be able to get her make-up just right. She'd made Koby set up the bright lights real photographers use, so she could test out her make-up techniques. Luckily, there were plenty of photographer's lights in the A/V Center at school.

With all of that preparation behind her, Jade felt confident as she strolled into the photographer's studio. She knew her make-up would work. She was also sure that her straight-straight-straight hairstyle with two thin, beaded braids framing either side of her head would give her an exotic, romantic image that none of the other contestants would be able to mimic.

"Oh, hi, you must be Jade," said a girl not much older than her. "We're almost ready for you. Why don't you take a seat over there by the make-up table and see if you want to do any touch-ups?"

"Are you the photographer?" Jade asked.

"No, I'm his assistant. I set up the lights, get him new rolls of film, coffee if he wants it."

"Oh," Jade said quietly.

"Hey, it's not as bad as it sounds," the girl joked.

"I'm a photography student. This is excellent training."

"I'm sure it is," Jade said.

"Come on, go check out your look in the mirror. You seem amazing to me, but I know you models are perfectionists about your make-up."

Jade beamed. This girl, who was practically a photographer, had called her a model. How cool was that?!

Jade walked over to the make-up mirror and studied her reflection. She smiled. Her make-up seemed perfect. But she reached into her bag and pulled out a little more lip gloss anyway, just to shine her lips up a bit.

A few minutes later, Jade found herself in front of the camera, smiling prettily as the photographer took shot after shot. She was surprised that the work was as difficult as it was. Professional models always made it seem so easy. But it was no easy task to remain cool under the hot lights. The photographer asked a lot of her, forcing her to hold uncomfortable positions for long periods of time, and telling her to keep smiling, and to keep her eyes wide open even as the wind machine made her tear up. Every now and then, the photographer's assistant would come over and powder down the shine on her face, or brush her windblown hair into place.

But the toughest part of the session came when the assistant entered the room with a large cage in her arms. She reached inside and pulled out a long, thick, brightly-colored snake. "What's that for?" Jade asked, eyeing the slithering reptile nervously.

"Don't worry," the assistant assured Jade. "The snake won't hurt you." She reached up and placed the big snake around Jade's neck like a giant, brightly-colored necklace.

It took everything Jade had not to scream as she felt the dry snakeskin slithering against the back of her neck. But she knew that the photographer was used to models who were willing to pose with snakes or puppies or babies to get their message across. *What I wouldn't do for a furry puppy right about now,* Jade thought ruefully. A professional model would be as friendly with that snake as she possibly could. And that was what Jade was going to do. She reached up and gently petted the snake's skin.

"That's perfect!" the photographer shouted from behind his lens. "Pet him again. Oh, Jade, you're a natural."

That was all the encouragement Jade needed. She immediately became more relaxed, stroking the snake's back, and even managing a giggle or two as the snake switched positions slightly, tickling her neck.

"Okay, that's it," the photographer said as he finished yet another roll of film. "Thanks for all the good work."

The photographer's assistant took the snake from Jade's neck. "You were great," she assured her. "Not all the girls have been so comfortable with Cicely here."

"Cicely?" Jade asked.

"That's her name."

"Oh, the snake's a girl," Jade murmured. She wasn't quite sure how you could tell, but she decided to take her word for it.

"Some of the girls were downright petrified," the assistant said. "But you seemed like you'd been around snakes all your life. I think those shots are going to be amazing—very exotic."

"Why did he photograph me with a snake?" Jade asked.

"It was sort of a test," the assistant explained. "The judges will want to know just how badly you want this gig.

A real model has to be ready for anything."

Jade nodded. A test. Just as she'd suspected. Luckily, she'd obviously passed with flying colors. "When do I get to see the photos?" she asked.

"On Saturday. We'll unveil your best shot at the contest."

"I don't get to pick my favorite?"

The assistant shook her head. "Your job's done. It's not up to you to pick which one works the best."

"You mean I have no control over which photo is entered in the contest?"

The assistant laughed. "Very few models have any say in which photos of them are used. The photographers and the magazine editors choose the ones that send the message they have in mind. But don't worry, I don't think there's a bad shot on that roll. You were great!"

Jade frowned slightly as she walked out of the studio. She only hoped the photographer's assistant was right.

■ ■ ■ ■

Cloe's photo session was the last of the ten. She didn't get to the photographer's studio until Friday afternoon. Jade had seen Cloe in school before then, of course, and she'd mentioned how well her photo session had gone. But she'd pointedly not mentioned any of the specifics—especially the snake test. What would be the point of giving her competitor a heads up? Instead, she'd chatted about homework, the big test coming up in art history, and how bad the food at lunch had gotten recently.

Which explained why Jade felt a bit guilty when she arrived at the contest on Saturday afternoon. She knew that, had Cloe been given a warning about coming face-to-face with the snake, she could have prepared herself.

But, surprisingly, Cloe didn't seem the least bit upset by the snake incident. In fact, she was practically glowing when she talked about wearing a real snake around her neck. "Wasn't that exciting, Jade?" she remarked. "I mean, it was the most beautiful thing I'd ever seen. And the funny thing was, the green dress I was wearing matched the green in the snake's body perfectly. You'd have thought I'd planned it."

Jade forced a smile to her lips, and tried to remember that Cloe wasn't just her competition, she was her friend, as well. "I'm sure your photos turned out great, Angel," she said, trying to sound genuinely pleased for her pal.

Just then, the woman with the red lipstick appeared in front of a giant screen that had been set up at the front of the store. "Okay, ladies, we're ready to get started," she announced. "We've got a very impressive panel of judges here. Each one of them is the editor of a major teen magazine. They know what they're talking about when it comes to critiquing photographs. Now I know that you're all anxious to find out how your photos came out. And I can't bear to make you wait a moment longer."

At that moment, someone in the back of the store turned out the lights, and the photos of the ten contestants appeared on a huge white screen. There was an audible gasp as each of the girls caught sight of their image for the first time. The photographer had certainly done his job—there wasn't a bad photo in the bunch.

But that didn't mean that each of the photos was a winner. Some of the girls seemed stiff, and their smiles not quite genuine. On the other hand, some of the girls were truly naturals; their poses could appear on the cover of any magazine in the country.

Jade hoped her photo was in the latter category. The photographer had chosen a shot of her laughing as the brightly-colored snake wriggled around on her skin. She looked completely full of joy. She was glad that she'd gone with an exotic look for her make-up, and had added some extra color to her lips. The result was a photo that popped out from the crowd in a burst of color.

Cloe spotted her photo right away, as well. Although she and the snake had gotten along very well, the photographer had chosen a picture of Cloe that registered her surprise when the animal was first placed around her neck. Her blue eyes were wide open, and her rich full lips were opened slightly, as though she had just murmured "oh." The result was a photograph of a girl with amazing vulnerability mixed with fierce determination.

After giving the girls time to fully examine their photos, and to compare them to the shots taken of the other girls, the woman with the red lipstick returned to the front of the room. The lights were turned back on. "You all did an amazing job," she assured the girls. "It was very difficult for our judges to choose between you all. But, as you know, only five girls can move on to our final competition."

Jade could barely breathe. There were at least six photos up there which were, in her opinion, genuine winners. And, of course, hers was one of them. But that still left her a one-in-six chance of not making it to the next round.

Time seemed to go very slowly as the woman with the red lipstick droned on and on about the difficulty of choosing winners for this round, and how she didn't doubt for a moment that all of the girls could someday go on to modeling careers if that was what they chose to do.

Just say the names, Jade thought silently. *Do it already.*

"Okay, I won't keep you waiting any longer," the woman with the red lipstick said. For a moment, Jade thought she'd accidentally spoken out loud. But one look at the faces of the other contestants, and she knew they'd all been thinking the exact same thing. The looks on their faces were like a massive telepathic message, broadcasting their need to be put out of their stressed-out misery.

"Here are our judges' choices for the five finalists. Our first finalist is . . . Cloe."

Cloe leaped up in the air excitedly. She ran up to the front of the room, and turned to smile at Jade. Jade managed to return her grin—while still listening for her name. But Jade didn't hear her name called next. Or even after that. Or after that. By the time Cloe and three other girls were standing together at the front of the room, Jade's heart was pounding madly. The last round had been so easy. She'd been called first. But now . . . there was actually a chance that she wouldn't be part of the final competition. And that thought was too hard to bear. Of course she was happy for Cloe, but . . .

"And our fifth and final contestant is . . . Jade!" the woman with the red lipstick announced.

Jade stood there for a moment, making sure she'd heard correctly. Then she let out a big sigh—she hadn't realized it, but she'd been holding her breath for an awfully long time. Quickly, Jade raced to the front of the room and took her place beside Cloe and the other finalists.

"We'll see you five girls back here for the final

competition, ready to model outfits you've put together yourselves," the woman with the red lipstick announced. "Remember, you have two weeks to put together something incredibly special."

Cloe and Jade looked over at each other. They managed to smile, even though both girls could sense an overwhelming competitive feeling coming over them. This could very well be the toughest two weeks of their lives.

chapter seven

Choosing an outfit that makes a statement isn't as easy as the girls made it look—especially if that outfit would determine whether or not you become the spokesmodel for a really cool boutique in the mall. Both Jade and Cloe put a lot of thought into their outfits. So much thought, in fact, that Sasha, Yasmin, Koby, Dylan, and Cameron hardly got to see them at all in the days that followed the photography competition. Jade and Cloe were too busy shopping and searching their closets looking for the outfit that would be a winner.

The gang finally did get together, however, on the Wednesday night before the contest. Their English teacher, Mr. O'Shea, gave them no choice. He assigned them a huge test for Thursday morning. That meant they had to get together for an emergency study session. They decided to meet at Jade's house. She provided the best eats.

"Doesn't Mr. O'Shea know that we have something far more important on our minds?" Cloe asked Jade as she plopped down on the couch in Jade's living room.

"I know. School's such a distraction," Jade agreed.

"Do you guys have your outfits all picked out?" Sasha asked.

"Almost," Cloe said excitedly. "I just have to see if I can find a pair of boots that work with my skirt."

Jade perked up immediately. "Oh, so you're wearing a skirt."

Cloe's face turned beet red. She hadn't wanted to reveal anything about her outfit before the big day. "I . . . um . . . didn't say that," she mumbled.

"Hey, can we get down to studying?" Koby butted in.

"Yeah. I'm just about ready to work," Cameron agreed.

"Just about?" Yasmin asked.

"I need some fuel first," he explained. "I like to think of my body as a finely-tuned car. I need to fill up my engine before I can make my brain work."

Jade laughed. "No prob, Cam. I've got the eats ready in the kitchen."

"Do you have any extra pencils?" Cloe asked her. "Mine all have broken points."

"Sure, they're upstairs in my desk."

"I'll get them," Cloe volunteered. "You get the munchies together."

It took a few minutes, but, eventually, everyone had a sharp pencil and a huge chocolate chip cookie in hand. The studying could finally begin.

■ ■ ■ ■

The study session at Jade's house went on long into the night. By the time Cloe dropped her friends off at their houses and pulled her convertible into her own garage, she was too tired to think of anything—not even which boots matched her skirt, or whether or not she should try out the new blue mascara before Saturday.

Still, somehow, she managed to pull herself out of bed on Thursday morning. When she got to school, she found Yasmin and Sasha on the front steps of the building, getting in a few last-minute looks at their notebooks.

"Hey, Angel, do you have a copy of the notes we

took last Monday?" Sasha called out to her. "I think I left mine at Jade's last night."

Cloe opened her notebook. "Special for you, Bunny Boo," she replied as she took the page out of her binder and handed it to her friend.

"Man, am I beat," Yasmin moaned. "That study session totally cut in to my beauty sleep."

"I know. It was like a sleepover party without the party," Cloe agreed. She looked around. "Did Jade go in to class already?"

Sasha shook her head. "Kool Kat hasn't made her arrival yet."

"I hope she doesn't oversleep and miss the test," Yasmin added. "We did kind of leave her with a mess to clean up last night. You think she stayed up too late?"

"Maybe," Cloe said. "But she made it, anyway." She pointed to the sidewalk in front of the school. Jade was on her way. She looked frantic.

"Relax, Jade," Yasmin called out to her. "You've still got five minutes before the bell."

Jade raced up to the school steps, her eyes blazing

and her cheeks red. "I don't care about some stupid test!" she shouted. "I've got much bigger problems."

"What could be a bigger problem than one of O'Shea's slammers?" Sasha asked. "His tests are the worst."

"Forget the test, wouldya," Jade moaned. "My outfit's gone!"

"What outfit?" Yasmin asked.

"What do you mean what outfit?" Jade demanded. "My outfit for the contest. It's gone. I spent a week-and-a-half putting together that look. And I spent a fortune on my blouse. And now everything's disappeared."

"Everything?" Sasha asked, suddenly alarmed.

"My jeans, my blouse . . . everything!" Jade exclaimed. "Except my boots. But I can't wear boots and nothing else, can I?"

"Oh, so you're wearing jeans," Cloe interrupted. She was happy to know one of Jade's secrets. Now they were even.

"Don't sound so surprised," Jade told her.

"Sorry," Cloe apologized. She draped one arm around Jade's shoulder and tried to comfort her. "Look, relax.

The clothes have to be somewhere. They couldn't have just disappeared."

"You're right," Jade agreed, wriggling away from Cloe's touch. "They didn't just disappear. You stole them!"

Cloe's eyes filled with tears. "I did not!" she insisted. "I would never do that to you—or to anyone."

Jade shook her head. "You knew you wouldn't be able to win on your own. You stole my outfit so you could walk off with the contest."

"That's ridiculous," Sasha butted in. "When would she have done that?"

"Last night!" Jade told her.

"How? We were all in the same room all night," Sasha reminded her.

"That's not true," Jade said. "She went upstairs to get pencils, remember? She could have easily shoved my jeans and blouse into her backpack without us noticing. That's probably why she didn't take the boots. We would have seen that."

Yasmin thought about that for a moment. All the clues did seem to lead to Cloe. But she couldn't believe for a moment that Cloe would ever do such a thing. Call it reporter's instinct, or maybe it was just that she'd read too many mystery novels, but Yasmin knew that the person you suspected most was usually not the culprit. "Oh, Jade, you don't really believe that," she said finally.

"Yes, I do," Jade insisted. Then she turned to Cloe. "But I'm going to win anyway." She spun on her platform heels and stomped into the school.

"That's what you think!" Cloe yelled after her. Then she ran to the bathroom and slammed the door.

That left Sasha and Yasmin standing there alone on the stairs, watching as their friends took off in opposite directions.

"You don't think Cloe would do something like that, do you?" Sasha asked Yasmin nervously.

"Never." Yasmin shook her head vehemently. "But Jade sure does."

"We've got to find out what happened to those clothes," Sasha told her. "Before this turns into a feud that can never be fixed."

Yasmin nodded. "I'm already on the case."

chapter eight

"I'm so glad you could come with me today, Pretty Princess," Cloe told Yasmin. "I really needed to relax after that whole mess with Jade this morning."

"Not to mention Mr. O'Shea's killer exam," Yasmin sighed. "I swear that man sits up at night coming up with ways to torment innocent high school students."

"Oh, don't make me laugh," Cloe said, choking back a giggle. "I'll crack this mud mask."

Yasmin nodded. The girls were chillin' out at the local Salon 'N' Spa. At the moment, they were soaking their feet in a warm pedicure bath, while their green mud masks hardened on their faces.

"I'm sure glad the judges can't see me now," Cloe joked. "Somehow, I don't think this is the look they're going for."

"I know," Yasmin said. "I'm kind of glad no one's here but us right now."

"Me, too," Cloe agreed. "I need to just get away from it all. I felt so awful today. How could Jade think I would do anything so terrible?"

Yasmin shrugged. "She's just nervous about the contest. She's not thinking straight. Don't worry. When she really thinks about it, she'll realize you could never do anything so mean."

"I don't think she'll ever get over it," Cloe argued. "She's too mad. The only way we'll ever get past this is if she finds those clothes. And I wouldn't begin to know where to start looking for them. I don't even know what she planned on wearing."

"Well, we still have this evening and all day tomorrow to find them," Yasmin reminded her.

Just then, two other girls walked into the room. Like Cloe and Yasmin, their faces were covered in green mud masks. They sat down in the two empty seats and placed their feet into tubs of warm, sweet-smelling water. For a while, the room was quiet. Then one of the new girls began to speak.

"Can you believe what she did to me?" one of them said to the other.

Cloe gasped. She'd know that voice anywhere. The girl behind the green face mask was Jade!

"You don't know that for sure," the other girl replied. Cloe's eyes widened. That was Sasha.

"Hey, that's . . ." Yasmin began.

"Shhh . . ." Cloe whispered in her ear. She knew that if Jade knew it was her and Yasmin behind their masks, she'd start another argument. And that was the last thing Cloe wanted right now.

"Come on, Bunny Boo, think," Jade moaned. "Who else could have done it? Who else would have *wanted* to do it?"

Sasha didn't have an answer for that. "I know it looks like Cloe's guilty, but . . ."

"No buts about it," Jade interrupted. "I know she stole my outfit. And I'll never forgive her for it. It was the most incredible look. I searched everywhere for just the right jeans. They were perfect: low-slung stretch jeans—the kind that really move with you and cling where they're supposed to. And I spent so much time putting pink, white, and purple rhinestone studs on them—it took me hours to get it just right. But I had to have the studs because they matched the smaller rhinestones that trim the red off-the-shoulder peasant blouse I'd picked out." She sighed. "And I got it all done early, because I'd wanted to ask Koby to take a few test pictures for me, just to make sure everything looked perfect. Now I'm just going to have to throw something else together and hope for the best."

"You'll find some funky fashion," Sasha assured her. "And you'll be struttin' in style down that runway."

"I want to win that contest more than ever," Jade confided.

"Come on, Jade, it's just a competition."

"Just?!" Jade demanded.

Sasha nodded. "If you don't stop accusing Cloe, you're liable to lose something a lot more important."

"That friendship's already gone," Jade assured her. "How can you be friends with someone you don't trust?"

That was all Cloe could take. She popped up out of her chair. Unfortunately, she forgot that her feet were still soaking in the footbath. She tripped and fell to the floor, splashing water everywhere. A big piece of her face mask flew from her face and landed right on Jade's salon robe.

"That's it!" Cloe shouted as she scrambled to her feet. "I can't take it anymore. I didn't steal your outfit. I don't have to steal to win. Ever since this contest started, you've been trying to start a fight. That's what you're doing now. I've had enough of it. I'm going to end this thing once and for all." And, with that, she stormed out of the room.

Yasmin stared at Jade. "Now see what you've done!"

"Me?" Jade asked her. "What did I do?"

■ ■ ■ ■

That night, the friends were burning up the phone lines. Sasha, Yasmin, Koby, Cam, and Dylan were trying to come up with some way to salvage Cloe and Jade's friendship. But like the missing clothes, the answer to that problem was very elusive.

"I've been calling Cloe all night," Cam told Dylan. "She won't answer the phone."

"Maybe she's got caller ID," Dylan teased.

"Very funny," Cameron moaned. "I'm serious.

I have to talk to her. I feel like this whole thing's my fault."

"Your fault?" Dylan asked. "How can this be your fault . . . unless. No. It couldn't be. I mean, you wanted Cloe to win, but you wouldn't . . . would you?"

"NO!!!!!!!!!" Cameron shouted so loud he hurt Dylan's ear.

"Well, you do have a motive," Dylan said slowly.

Cameron was so mad, he didn't even know what to say. Instead, he slammed the phone down, hard.

A few minutes later, the phone rang at Sasha's house. She and Yasmin were in Sasha's bedroom. Sasha put the phone on speaker and answered the call. "Hello?"

"Bunny Boo, we got big problems," Koby said.

"That's the understatement of the year," Sasha replied.

"No, I'm not kidding," Koby said. "It's worse than you think. Now Dylan and Cam aren't speaking, either."

"What?" Sasha shouted, her voice climbing the scales nervously.

"Apparently, Dylan told Cam that he suspected him of committing the crime," Koby explained.

"We don't even know there was a crime committed," Yasmin butted in. "There are a lot of rational explanations about where those clothes could've gotten to."

"Name one, Pretty Princess," Koby demanded.

Yasmin sighed. She wished she were as great a detective as the ones in the mystery novels she always had her nose in. But the truth is, she wasn't. She was as clueless as the rest of her friends about where those clothes were.

Just then, there was a beep on the phone line. "That's my call-waiting," Sasha told Koby. "I'll call you back later."

"Okay," Koby answered. "Catch ya later." He hung up his phone.

Sasha hit the call-waiting button on her line. "Hello?"

"Bunny Boo, you've got to do something!" Cameron's voice insisted on the other end.

"I just heard about Dylan," Sasha told him. "I'm sorry, Cameron."

"I didn't steal her clothes. I didn't even know what she was wearing. And even if I did, who could find them in her room? She's got clothes everywhere. Her room is more cluttered than that clothing storage space she calls a locker. And that thing's a disaster."

Sasha laughed despite herself. "Look, just try to calm down. We'll get to the bottom of this."

"I sure hope so," Cameron replied.

As Sasha hung up with Cam, she let out a nervous sigh. She only wished she was as confident as she sounded. But the truth is, she wasn't sure this was a problem that could ever be fixed.

chapter nine

The next morning, Jade, Yasmin, and Dylan were all sitting on the front steps of the school. Jade and Dylan were in the midst of a very heated discussion.

"I think Cameron's really the one who did it," Dylan told Jade. "You should have heard him last night. He could barely even deny it. He just slammed the phone down." Dylan rubbed his ear. "I can still hear it."

Jade shook her head wildly. "No way. He might have the motive, but he didn't have the opportunity. Cloe did."

Dylan looked at her suspiciously. "Maybe they were in on it together. What if Cameron planned it out, and Cloe executed the plot?"

Yasmin stared at her two friends. "Will you listen to yourselves?" she demanded. "You make this sound like the crime of the century."

"It is to me," Jade told her honestly.

Before Yasmin could answer, Cloe, Sasha, and Cameron came walking up the path to the high school.

"What's Sasha doing with *them*?" Jade asked. "Don't tell me she's siding with Cloe now?"

"Sasha's not siding with anyone," Yasmin assured her. "She and I don't think there should be any sides to choose from."

Cloe, Sasha, and Cameron stopped in front of the others.

"I'm getting out of here," Jade said, quickly gathering up her books and turning to leave.

"Jade, calm down," Sasha said. "You don't know what Cloe has to say."

Jade looked at the huge garment bag Cloe held in her arms. "Unless she's here to tell me that she's got my outfit in that bag, I don't want to hear it."

Cloe shook her head. "I don't have your outfit in here," she said. "But I do have something for you." She held out the bag. Jade refused to take it.

"Oh, go ahead, Kool Kat," Sasha urged her quietly. She turned to Jade. "She worked on it all night."

Finally, Jade took the bag from Cloe's arms, and began to unzip it. "I'm only doing this to satisfy you, Bunny Boo," Jade said.

"Whatever it takes," Sasha agreed.

Jade reached inside the bag, and carefully removed the garment inside. Her eyes bugged when she saw the funky fashion within . . . a short white miniskirt with hundreds of tiny hand-painted paw prints all over it. The skirt was matched with a halter top. A kitten face with glowing blue eyes had been painted on the halter.

"Oh, wow!" Yasmin gasped.

"Unbelievable," Dylan agreed.

Jade was speechless. Finally, she found her voice. "You made this for me?" she asked.

Cloe nodded. "I didn't steal your clothes, Jade," she assured her. "But I didn't want you to be mad at me forever. I knew you didn't have much time to put together what you really wanted, and I wanted us both to look great on Saturday. It only took me one night . . ."

Jade looked from the outfit to Cloe and back again. Her cheeks began to burn red. "I can't take these," she said, handing the outfit back to Cloe.

"Oh, no, you're not still mad?" Cloe asked, seeing the hot red burning in Jade's face.

Jade shook her head. "Just embarrassed," she assured Cloe. "Now I know you couldn't have stolen my clothes. But I can't take this outfit. It's a guaranteed winner. And after all I've done to you, I can't beat you at the contest in your own outfit."

Cloe laughed. Same old Jade. "Oh, don't worry about that," Cloe assured her. "I've got somethin' just as sizzlin' back in my closet."

"I'll bet you do, Angel." Jade took Cloe by the hand. "Come on. Let's store this in my locker until after school." The girls walked inside together with Sasha, Yasmin, Dylan and Cameron close behind. "You know, I was thinking," Jade continued as they strolled down the hall. "I could add a little blue Funk 'N' Glow to my hair to match the kitten's eyes."

Cloe nodded. "A little hair flair never hurts."

Jade stopped at her locker. Quickly, she turned the dial on her lock. The locker door popped open and . . . suddenly a landslide of clothes poured out. In an instant, there were funky fashions all over the floor. "Oh, no," Jade groaned. "I did it again."

"You really need to clean out this locker," Sasha said as she began to help Jade fold the clothes that were strewn all over the floor. "I don't know how you've any room for books in here."

"Oh, are you supposed to keep books in there?" Jade laughed.

Sasha picked up a pair of hot-pink leather pants. "Can I borrow these?" she asked.

"Anytime," Jade assured her.

"This blouse is hot!" Cloe said, holding up a bright yellow half shirt with orange fringe sewn on the bottom.

"But not as hot as this one," Yasmin said, lifting up a red off-the-shoulder peasant blouse with rhinestone trim.

Jade stared at the blouse in shock. "My shirt!" she exclaimed.

"And check out these jeans," Yasmin continued. She held up the low-slung stretch jeans Jade had decorated with multi-colored rhinestone studs. "Isn't this the outfit you put together for the contest?"

"They were in my locker?" Jade exclaimed with surprise.

Yasmin nodded. "Apparently."

"But how . . ." Jade began. Then she stopped herself. "Oh, now I remember."

"Remember what?" Cameron asked her.

"I wanted Koby to take my picture after school on Wednesday, so I brought the outfit in. I stashed it in my locker, until I had a chance to ask him. But then Mr. O'Shea announced that test, and I forgot all about it." She turned to Cloe and Cameron. "I'm so sorry, you guys. This was all my fault."

Cloe and Cameron couldn't argue with that. Besides, what would be the point? Cloe reached out and gave Jade a hug. "It's cool," she assured her.

"We're still friends?" Jade asked cautiously.

"The best," Cloe assured her.

"But, you guys, Jade still has a big problem," Yasmin interrupted.

"What now?" Dylan asked her.

"Deciding which outfit she's going to wear on Saturday!"

"She's going to wear her sizzlin' studded outfit, of course," Cloe answered.

"But she'd look purr-fect in that cat look you created," Cameron told Cloe.

"So what are you going to wear?" Sasha asked Jade.

Kool Kat gave her a mysterious smile. "You'll all have to wait and see."

chapter ten

On Saturday morning, Cloe was a nervous wreck. She'd arrived at the contest early so she would have plenty of time to get ready. She'd figured Jade would've done the same, but here it was, just fifteen minutes before the contest, and there was still no sign of Jade.

The backstage area was a complete madhouse. There were only five girls left in the contest, and only four were there so far, but it seemed like there were a hundred, what with all the blow-dryers buzzing, the make-up brushes flying, and the hangers being strewn all over the floor. Despite all the backstage noise, Cloe could still hear cheers coming from the next room, where the runway had been set up. The Unique Boutique had allowed an audience to come and cheer the girls on for the final round of the spokesmodel competition.

Cloe looked in the mirror and applied another

streak of sparkling silver eye shadow on both of her lids. The silver matched her outfit perfectly—she was wearing a dark blue denim minidress with streaks of silver hand-painted onto the fabric. The effect was electric—like lightning shooting across a night sky. Cloe had carried the blue-and-silver theme all the way through, from her head to her toes. On her feet were shimmering silver platform boots; her hair was parted into two long ponytails, one with a denim bow and the other with a silver one. No doubt about it, Cloe's look was sizzlin' with style.

Still, she wasn't completely comfortable in the outfit. Cloe's fave fashion passion was animal prints. And, for a while, she'd considered wearing a black-and-orange tiger-print skirt and top for the competition. But now that she'd given Jade the hand-painted cat outfit, well, she didn't want the judges thinking that either of them had been unoriginal. Still, standing there now in the dressing room, Cloe wasn't sure she'd made the right choice. If only Jade were there to let her know . . .

"Angel—that dress is awesome!"

Suddenly, Cloe heard Jade's voice shout out over

the din in the dressing room. She relaxed at the very sound of it. Cloe turned around to take a look at Jade. She wasn't the only one staring. All the girls in the room had stopped what they were doing long enough to check out the exotic beauty. It was impossible not to. Jade had put together an amazing outfit. She'd worn the hand-painted halter Cloe had created for her—but she'd dressed it up with a blue feather boa that matched the blue in the cat's eyes perfectly. Instead of the paw print miniskirt, Jade had gone with a pair of white leather jeans. She'd finished off her look with white platform boots.

"That outfit makes you look amazing," one of the other girls told Jade. She didn't bother to try and hide her jealousy.

"No, it doesn't," Cloe countered.

Jade stared at her. Was it possible Cloe really hadn't forgiven her after all? "It doesn't?" she asked cautiously.

"Of course not," Cloe replied. "You make the outfit look amazing!"

Jade grinned. Things really were back to normal between them. "So, Angel, are you ready for your runway debut?" she asked.

Cloe grimaced. "I'm not sure. I heard there were a lot of people out there."

"Yeah, but the only ones I care about are Sasha, Yasmin, Cameron, Dylan, and Koby. And they're right in the front row," Jade assured her. "They're here to cheer."

"Cheer for who?" Cloe asked.

"Both of us," Jade assured her. "And I'm rooting for us, too."

Just then, the woman with the red lipstick appeared in the doorway. "Okay, girls, this is it," she said. "Line up in the order posted on the wall. As soon as the music starts, it's time for the first girl on the list to hit the runway. Good luck to all of you."

Cloe was the second girl to take on the runway. She was nervous at first—but knowing her friends were out there allowed her to relax and have a good time. She winked at them as she passed by. When she reached the end of the runway, she twirled slowly, giving the judges a chance to view her outfit from every angle. It was amazing just how poised and professional she seemed.

Jade was the fourth girl to hit the catwalk.

She seemed to be having a blast out there—walking, grinning, and twirling with amazing energy. At one point, she bent down and playfully tickled the cheek of one of the judges with her feather boa. The judge went along with the gag, smiling and pretending to fall off his chair, laughing. The audience loved it.

Jade returned to the backstage area, confident that she had a good shot at winning the contest.

Then the final girl took to the stage. She too walked along the platform modeling her outfit. After she was finished, the contest was over. There was nothing left but the judging.

As the girls waited backstage for the final results, they were silent. The tension was palpable. One by one, the girls reached for powder and brushes, trying to cover the beads of nervous perspiration that were popping out on their faces. Cloe went over and stood beside Jade. The girls held hands, hoping that between them they would be able to gather enough courage to endure the horrible tension.

"I don't know how much more of this I can take," Cloe whispered to Jade.

"It's out of our hands now," Jade replied. "We just have to wait."

"And wait . . ." Cloe added. "And wait . . . and . . ."

"Would all the girls please come out onstage," the woman with the red lipstick called out into her microphone. She waited patiently as the girls made their way out in front of the audience. They were greeted with loud cheers from the audience.

"I agree," the woman with the red lipstick told the crowd. "These girls are all deserving of your praise. In my mind, they're all winners. But we can only have one spokesmodel."

Come on, Cloe thought to herself. *Just announce the winner.* She clasped her hands together, and was surprised when her palms were damp and clammy. She forced a smile to her lips. For the first time, Cloe realized just how badly she wanted to win the contest.

But no matter how badly Cloe wanted to win, Jade wanted it more. Ever since she'd been a little girl, she'd wanted to model. And now her chance to do just that was finally within reach. All that stood between her and the chance of a lifetime were four other girls. One of whom just happened to be one of her closest friends.

Which, of course, complicated things.

To the outside world, Kool Kat was living up to her nickname. She seemed cool, calm, and collected. She was smiling brightly and staring right into the eyes of the judges. But it was all an act. Inside, Jade was wilting under the pressure. Her head felt light, and everything around her seemed to be going in slow motion. Her heart was pounding. For a moment, she thought she might faint, so she forced herself to breathe slowly through her nose.

"Okay, girls, I won't leave you in suspense a moment longer," the woman with the red lipstick said. "I have in my hands three envelopes. One has the name of the second runner-up. One has the name of our first runner-up—who will take over for the winner should she have to resign for any reason. The third envelope contains the name of the girl we have chosen to represent Unique Boutique."

Cloe looked down the line at all the girls. It was easy to tell that every one of them was hoping it was her name in that third envelope.

The woman with the red lipstick gingerly opened the first envelope. Time seemed to stand still. Finally, the woman read, "The second runner-up is . . . Cloe!"

Cloe gasped when she heard her name. Second runner-up. She wasn't quite sure what to feel. Getting that close to winning was definitely pretty good. Still, she couldn't help but feel a little let down.

The pressure was off Cloe now, but Jade was still feeling the heat. As Cloe stepped forward to receive her prize—a bouquet of roses and a gift certificate to the Unique Boutique—she glanced enviously at Jade. She still had a shot at being the winner. In fact, there was no doubt in her mind that Jade would be the spokesmodel.

Too bad Cloe wasn't one of the judges. Because at that moment, the woman with the red lipstick announced the first runner-up. "Jade!" she said excitedly.

Cloe knew Jade must be disappointed at not having won. But she was professional enough not to show it. The dark-haired beauty smiled brightly and waved to the audience as she stepped up to receive her prize. As bummed out as she was at not winning, Jade tried to remind herself that lots of famous models had had their share of disappointments before making it big.

When the name of the winner was finally called, Cloe and Jade both cheered for her. After all, there's nothing fashionable about a poor sport.

■ ■ ■ ■

"You guys were robbed," Dylan insisted as Cloe and Jade made their way off the stage and joined the rest of the girls. "You both should have won."

"We couldn't both win," Cloe told him.

"Well, one of you should've," Dylan said.

"Which one?" Jade asked him.

Dylan thought about that for a moment. There was no way he could choose between the girls. "Come to think of it, maybe things worked out for the best," he admitted.

"Besides, we both got $100 gift certificates to the Unique Boutique," Cloe said. "That's a nice prize."

"I'll say," Jade agreed. "I think I'll use part of mine to get that black-and-white hoodie I saw."

"Hey, wait a minute, I was going to get that,"

Cloe interrupted.

"You can't. I saw it first."

"No way. It was the first thing I noticed when I walked into the store."

"Prove it!"

Quickly, Sasha stepped between the two girls to keep them from starting up a fresh argument.

"Here we go again," she giggled.

"No way," Jade assured her. "We're never going to fight again."

"How about you get the hoodie, and I get the black jeans with the white stripe?" Cloe suggested. "Then we can share the outfit."

"And we never have to worry about wearing the same thing on the same day," Jade agreed. "Angel, you're a genius!"

"I won't argue with that," Cloe laughed as she reached over and gave her friend a big hug.